T0339709

missing

missing

First published by Modjaji Books, Cape Town, 2010.
Second edition published by Modjaji Books, Cape Town, 2014.
This edition published by Dryad Press, Cape Town, 2019.

Dryad Press (Pty) Ltd
Postnet Suite 281, Private Bag X16, Constantia, 7848, Cape Town
www.dryadpress.co.za

Cover design: Stephen Symons
Editor: Michèle Betty
Typography: Stephen Symons
Set in 9.5/14pt Palatino Linotype
Photograph of Beverly Rycroft: Shawn Benjiman

ISBN: 978-0-6398091-0-6

missing

BEVERLY RYCROFT

DRYAD PRESS
People! Read Poetry

CONTENTS

For John
and for Ben, Georgia and Emma

Homing

for Ben

Fifteen years of marriage,
sixteen different houses.

On moving days her whining Bernina
gobbled curtains, sheets, name tags;
tattooed new uniforms with old labels,
(the rippings of previous stitches
still dangling like milk teeth).

He set up the loft.

Reassembled it in each new garden,
satellite to mother-ship,
decanted (again) its freight
of brewing, scratching birds.

Family holidays up the coast,
Dad would stop the car
near Komga, Berlin, Middledrift.

We three knew how to pin wings
with our hands,
how to push a bird
to the patient air.

We liked to stand and watch them circle
then stitch, unerring as needles,
through the silky sky towards
wherever home was then.

Love was a Red Datnis Bakkie

Love was a red Datnis bakkie
we weren't allowed to drive.

We drove it anyway.
You knew that.

Weekdays after school
we'd gun it down
the Albert Road driveway,
clipping the fender,
ruining the clutch.

You knew that too.

We'd hide. You'd catch us.
Roar *What the hell,*
full-throttle fifth gear round the
bloody bend. Smoking language
that piled up over
our house
our yard
the whole of
King William's Town.

Oh Dad your tales of our cunning
and deception,
our daring
and devious ways.

You never taught us but
we learned to drive that truck.
Only a matter of time
– you knew damn well –
before we learned to slide

clutch in
brake out,
gear shifts that matched
our incomprehension,
     your irony. Reverse speeding
down the long drive till finally
we turned to put foot
     out
through the open gate.

Living in a Shoe

See saw marjory daw
out you all slid and needed feeding.

The nurses showed me how.

My nipple, your mouth.
That was the start of it.
There were rules, but I couldn't follow.
Not my language.

To me, every bird
was a witch in disguise,
every rat a coach driver.
In each white corridor
signs spun laughing

> *Forty miles to London*
> *This way first*
> *Follow me*
> *Drink this*

Reading them
I turned to stone.

Nights blazed.
I puzzled at your cries,
crazy with the quest.
A million sounds, a million shapes
to match them to until

finally
defeated
I turned to the only magic I knew,

the shapeless, angry
loving you.

House of Cards

Months before it happened
Heather held a party
at her Victorian semi in Obs.

Women only.

She'd invited a Tarot reader.

There was the usual fare:
good food
wine
high-class coffee.

It was a chance to see
what her other friends had been doing
since I saw them last.

I was always a curious child.

One
by one
we were invited into
the other room
where the unseen woman dealt her cards.

I wouldn't go.

1997

Nothing foretold that year.
No hint from the *Cape Times* horoscope
or a *Fair Lady* flipped through at
the dentist's waiting room.

(Strong winds,
they might have whispered,
gale force hurricanes.
Be good to those around you.)

Meanwhile the world rebuilt itself
in twenty-four-hour shifts.
I clocked in for treatment
and waited, treading water,
never certain
what I was waiting for.

It may have been
the wild comet we woke to see one morning.
From the steadiness of our cold, dark lawn
the wind leaped up in recognition.
It blurred our cotton nightgowns
as your grandmother and I
pointed out the ripped sky.
In your striped pyjamas
you were just grown past my waist.

The world
essentially
was as it always had been
(as the comet tore past, a bullet-train),
and the stars stayed where they'd always stood,
as though pounded through concrete
with sledge-hammers of steel.

Filofax

Someone toppled a tree
and flailed it bare for me.
Broke its rounded neck
and savaged it to squares.

January February March,
between those thin black lanes
my wild hand entered,
steering a pen.

Monday Tuesday Friday after next

I toured the future
decreeing your destinies.
Ballet karate toddler's gym
perfect teeth perfect sight perfect hair perfect skin.

April May and finally

June
Friday 30th
Eleven am

Doctor's appointment.

At my fingertips your names lie
like dead-headed roses.

On the blank pages ahead
months
years
drained of my signature.

Thursday: Mammogram

Is this a true picture does it
give a good likeness
did you get my left side
it is better than my right?
Like the portrait painters of old have you
exaggerated my eyes – compensated
for an overbite?

Stand still please.
The camera does not lie.
We will capture you
just as the world sees you,
no better, no worse.
Move left please.
A little higher. A little
closer to the machine.

There.

Now we have you.

Friday: Diagnosis

The telephone, once a domestic creature,
has turned into a raptor.
At nine last night it sprang, the first attack.
The doctor's voice spinning from it
steamed warm and sticky
as fresh entrails:
malignancy
chemotherapy

Cancer.

When I dropped the receiver back the shriek
became a burr again.

This morning it perches
beside my unmade bed,
wings folded, eyes shut
feigning sleep.

Saturday: Spreading the News

The colour of the grass is green
the colour of the sky is blue
Georgia's hair is blonde
it shines in the sun.

Georgia's father is John
he wears a red shirt
John is walking across the green grass
to tell Granny.

John is the magic man he
wades through the colours and
the colours don't know or even
suspect the words he is smuggling
down their pretty path.

Can you see me?
I'm at the lounge window.
I'm watching John as he
walks down the path and
carries the words
to give Granny.

The grass is green today
the sky is very blue
Georgia's hair is blonde
John's shirt is red
Granny wears a pink dress

The words
are black and white.

Monday: Nil per Mouth

Monday morning
nil per mouth.
Book in at eight and
they'll take it out
take it off
take it away.

All weekend you feel it
crouched inside your breast.
You can smell its hot nest.
Over its sleepless gobble
your thin skin trembles.

Monday they'll do it.
The surgeons will step up
scrub up
snap on gloves.

Once and for all
they're going to rid you
of this turbulent breast.

Note to my Surgeon

Measure carefully.
Consider well.
Whatever you choose to leave behind
becomes all that remains

of me.

Superwoman

Meat and flies obeyed her. Water changed state.
The kettle, bulging silver, boiled and grew
into a mirror. Her tiny double flew
across its sky, a sabred warrior caped
in home-sewn dressing gown. Superwoman!
Samurai! One cleave of that cutlass could
carve any carrot, trim any onion,
slice, spread and banish that butter to bread.

We're in room sixteen, surgical ward, where
kryptonite-green gloves spring open all
the precision-made parts that brought her here.
The kidney-tray's a curving silver screen
to echo blades that whisper through her skin
split wide to track the saboteur within.

Household Magician

You made 'em laugh, alright. Played both ringmaster
and clown. But magic was your greatest act,
the table with the tall, black hat. You lifted it,
Shazaam! A pink-eyed rabbit, white shanks a-quiver!
He'd crouch there, staring. Only he could see
beyond them: the crowd you'd tamed
and shrunk, small enough to trap in the circle
of your greasy, sweating palm.

Tonight, unmasked, you sleep – yourself again.
But what's this ladder? This taut rope, this wire?
The crowd's drugged eyes now magnetised higher.
You only knew this prospect from below,
yet the one that must cross that line, must toe
that wire – and you're not dreaming now – it's You.

Room Thirteen

I married a gambling man.

Lucky for some,
he says as I
thread my body through
the green gown
in room thirteen.

No jewellery, the nurses order, so
I hand him
my wedding ring. Eleven years married
I'm wheeled away to

wake up again in room thirteen,
broad bandage across my chest.

He's still there. Slides the ring back
on. Tells me

It's not the hand you get dealt.
It's the way you play it.

What I Learned from You

Initially, I learned
nothing
from you.

That was because I already knew everything.

I knew how to drive a car with the seatbelt clipped on
and keep to the speed-limit,
I knew how to make the bed *before* I left for work,
how to plan for supper each night,
to switch off the verandah light before we went to bed
and
astonishingly
how to change a roll of toilet paper.

In time it became clear.
There were some things you could show me.

For instance,
how not to be the first to leave a party,
how to sleep with the windows open,
how to persuade a child to taste smoked snoek pâté
and how to find a winner for
the Saturday afternoon pick-six at Kenilworth.

It's true. You taught me
that a bad taste in ties is neither terminal
nor contagious
and a brown gomma-gomma bedroom suite
isn't the worst way to start a marriage.

From you I learned to dance rock 'n roll on a hotel lawn,
to sing along
– in public –
to a Neil Diamond CD,
to step back and allow a boy to become a man,
but that every grown man with a cold
wants only his mama.

You taught me that no amount of Pres-Stik will fix
a broken garden gate,
how to blame someone else
when I lose my keys,
and how, if we really had to,
you and I might just manage
without each other.

Rock Paper Scissors

Rock
(I take a photo on our honeymoon)

One in each hand
you on the Paxos beach
white rocks
blue sea
and you
interrupting the landscape.

Paper
(In the doctor's rooms I look at you)

The skin below your eyes
flimsy as the pathology
notes floating to the surface
of the doctor's
yellow file.

Scissors
(You wish it had happened to someone else)

I think they used a knife.
I would have preferred
the companionable kissing of scissors,
the high-legged can-can of twin blades
through the deviant tissue
of my breast.
As if they were cutting paper dolls
for a birthday cake
or lining for a wedding-gown
of mulberry-tinted silk.

Water

Water goes
where gravity commands.

Today (your first shower since) –
it no longer arcs over that grape-shaped globe,
that Picasso curve, as it used to,
season after fruitful season,
but gathers, fickle as fresh dew,
in this surprising new cliff,
this old-woman toothless mouth
puckered pink with defeat.

David's Visit

David arrives at my hospital room
with flowers in a sea-green pot.

He tells me,
in his Aunt's day,
breast prosthetics were bolstered
with bird-seed.

After a sweaty game of tennis
one afternoon, she found
her bosom had begun to sprout.

I wonder what bounty
the bald, pink grave of my breast
will offer up for harvest?

Petunias?
An armour-plated
rose beetle?
Bumbling bees searching foolishly for pollen?

Or a ravine
for a drought-stricken river
that until now
had given up all hope
of ever flowing through.

I'm not Afraid

I'm not afraid
of anaesthetic
or even surgery.
I'm not afraid of sleeping
in this stiff white bed
where nurses rub my back
and shelter me from
the minor illnesses next door.

I'm only afraid of my
baby's happy face
and the doctor's footsteps
drawing nearer
down the corridor.

Pathology Results

Green arrow. Ground floor. *Ping.*
The doors retreat,
yielding up the doctor.
She's set on course for me,
seated at the hospital canteen.

In her hand, a sheath of dead papers.

I can spy them from where I sit.
Observe, on their flinty surface,
how the words flap and curl
while the air slowly drowns them.

Lured and landed
they'll be gutted soon,
for my un-hungry eyes:
Positive
Metasteses
Spread.

I'd Like you to Look at your X-Rays

On the sixth floor we're almost eye level
with three white clouds that have strayed
into the maze of buildings
around Wynberg Hospital.

They've no language for
where they've been left,
lost, above the traffic
and hawkers selling fruit
and taxi drivers we can hear,
even from behind the double-glazed windows
of the doctor's room.

No one's forced me here.
I'm free if I wish to catch
– for five rand only –
a ride to
Rondebosch
Claremont
Mowbray
or Cape Town Central Station.

If I wanted I could take a train
to the east coast, disembark
at East London, hitch to Transkei.

I'm told long-horned Nguni cattle still bask
on the Wild Coast rocks,
and get called back each evening
by barefoot boys in school uniform.

I've seen for myself the clouds
that sprawl and slur untranslated
across that sky beneath which poverty
and death
are quite unremarkable.

Walking to School Again

We'll take the shortcut
like we always do.
Left along Mayfield,
then left into the lane
again.

This is the left hand,
this is the right.
For you, it's the one
you *write* with.

Hold my hand and look both ways.
Tell me about your test today,
and the raffle tickets we *must* sell,
and all the slips I haven't signed.

I'll try not to mention
– while you're talking –
the scar that's carved
its crooked detour
over my chest.

Ons sal Afrikaans praat.
Ons sal oefen vir die toets.

And you won't know
– 'cause I won't tell –
how at the corner
of Mayfield and Muir
the streets fall to their knees.

How I see him waiting on the corner
just for me,
in his smart white coat
with his white-gloved hands,
his smile rooting like a tumour.

But don't you worry.

I'll watch you cross.
I'll see you safe.
Promise to
meet you at two
by the big school gate.

I'll walk home
on my own, just
the way we came

no shortcuts
no detours
no dodging that corner
or the quiet chanting

Black white left right
Cross over now

of that lollipop man.

Mending

My mother could turn her hand
to anything (except cooking).
Kimberley Girls' High Dux Scholar,
East London City's top shorthand and typing pupil,
Border and district court stenographer.

Ample, steady, accurate,
her large hands could even dispense
a stern swipe at a bottom
or (once) a clean chop across the jaw
when father went too far.
Again.

She ploughed scissors through cloth,
pinned, tacked, sewed,
glued and weeded.

Not to worry, she'd say,
let's start again.
Everything will work out fine.

Decades later,
visiting America. The phone
like a dead baby in her palms.
Then plane after plane,
passports
customs
surly baggage men,
all undone by my mother
unpicking her way steadily back

towards the continent
the country
the city
the hospital-ward
where her husband finally ushers her,

the bed
where her daughter waits,
their eyes ambushing her
as if to say

Here's what's happened.
Fix it.

Grace by Name

Ferrying socks and underwear
down my southern suburbs
passageway, plastic basket
balanced primly on her head.
Madiba-like,
aloof
her wide hips taunt me,
White girl I've had troubles worse
than you will ever know
but you will never know them.

Sometimes,
as if they're corners she's
turned to dusting,
she knocks out for me
– disdainfully –
a memory or two.
Her mother, her daughter,
two nights in Wynberg jail
for travelling without a pass.

The magistrate he say I can go.
He say he can see I got
the white blood in me
because I speak the English well.
I tell him: not me.
***I** not got the*
white blood in me.
*Not **my** family.*

Then, *naughty Momma* she fumes,
arresting a passing child,
Why you not put the vest on the baby?
And, *You got the two children already,*
why you getting another baby now?

Tuesday morning,
home from hospital.
I limp into the kitchen,
my drip tucked neatly into
the pocket of my coat.

Looming up at me from
the dark sink,
hot dishwasher hands,
warm salt on my neck,

O my Dulling.
Why these things must be?

What Life is Really Like

You need to toughen up,
my father would complain
when I was small,
I ought to take you to see
chickens having their heads
chopped off.
That'd teach you
*what life is **really** like.*

He'd seek me out
when one of his pigeons
– crazed for home
or mad with terror from
a roaming hawk –
would tumble into the loft,
mutilated by wire or beak.

I was the one made
to clench my palms
around its pumping chest,
to keep it still
while my father's hairy fingers
stitched its garotted throat
angrily to rights again.

You see life is a fight for survival,
he'd shout, forgetting
he was not lecturing his students
or giving his inaugural address,
You gotta roll with the punches.
I waited and waited

for that bitter roughness
to spy me and circle in to land.
Years and years
of flinching anticipation
until the day I came home from hospital
and my father dressed my wound.

Easing with practiced hands
the drip from my bulldozed chest,
he renewed the plaster
in breathing silence
never speaking never once saying

Life's a bastard.
Toughen up.

Sticks And Stones

My father is stuck now in this wooden frame and cannot argue
any more. Once upon a time, the camera breathed the same air as
him and the shutter fell. That is the only connection. But
his words escaped. He breathed on them and they pulled his
breath in and sat up. They grew feet and walked. Then they
marched. Across our generation they trekked, indefatigable:
*What the bloody hell are you doing? You are killing me. Not like
that, stupid bastard.* Some set to chopping down trees and setting
up camp. They built cabins to house them forever in the territory
of our skinny minds. Others, instead of legs, sent out shoots,
green-tipped, to curl in at the nursery windows of the babies
we eventually brought before him. *For God's sake man,* was very
popular, and, in time, *Jesus Christ what have you done to my car?*
Yet others formed armies and marched on over the battlefields
of our scarred hills. *I am ashamed to call you son. You are nothing
like the daughter I wanted. No man will ever marry you.*
Some, weary of doing the same old thing, eventually retired in
the hollows of our creaking brains, where apartments were still
waiting to be filled. They settled there forever.
Those that stayed the course, grew softer, and overweight. They
broke ranks. Their hair spun out long and white, in clumps or
not at all. They forgot to shave. Bristles glinted like shattered
ice on their pliable jaws. Instead of leaping and marching, they
began to glide, then float. Wind-light, they submitted eventually
to capture. Finally they posted fragile, white postcards home:
Forgive me.
I love you.
I was always
so proud of you.

Hair

The least of my worries now
this charred field spanning my skull,
this noiseless shedding
of a million slim needles of hair
each time I lean in to the mirror.

What concerns me
is what's been hidden all these years.
This scar, for instance,
floated to the surface of my frontal lobe.
It slip-knots a memory:

a party
children
balloons

and sudden blood.

Dying Women Should Not Wear Lipstick

Dying women should not wear lipstick
or pink-checked mini skirts that shriek
Sexy! and shoot right up
past their skinny knees
towards their truncated breasts.
They ought not to wear
pillbox hats that lodge
on their stubbled heads
like stranded yachts, or put on
stiletto heels or shiny earrings,
or even oddly-matched shoes.
They must stay at home
and wear brown scarves.
They must turn their dying faces
away from the rest of us
and not eat ice cream
on Sea Point promenade
or enjoy spring, or breed hamsters.
They **may not** run
in the annual school sports day mothers' race
and definitely never win.

Of course they are allowed to cry.

But only in the privacy
of their own locked rooms,
and only when holding
a pillow over their warm
and dying mouths to stop
their children from knowing

there is something a little more
than dying going on in there.

If this Bed Could Talk

If this bed could talk
it would say,
Here you lay with him,
in this hollow,
worn there by the lying together,
the lying above, below,
the side by side of sleep.

It would say, *This island in the middle?*
Your youngest child colonised it
at midnight for years,
wanting only your tired hand,
burrowing for it like a mole
before she finally fell asleep.

At this end,
the bed would say,
your son (once a boy),
flung his sleeping bag on the floor
to bring out the night near both of you
after reading a horror story too late.

This bed would say,
Here, beside me,
your mother stood,
wearing your apron, saying
Please, eat something,
I will make anything if you would just eat.

And here sat your daughter,
singing nursery rhymes
while she stroked
your stubbled head.

And here,
the bed would sigh,
is evidence of how you have worn me out,
worried me away to barely nothing
through days and days of lying here.
Here, it would whisper,
in this hollow,
while they all slept,
you lay awake

Waiting.

The Youngest Brother

Tom would try anything once.
John Denver,
home-made koeksusters,
stealing chips from Dad's secret stash.

Where I saw bricked tower walls,
tall Tom lounged over and shook out,
like a washday sheet,
the landscapes he spied.
Sand-dunes, oceans,
summers on the Transkei coast,

and grew taller still.
Looked over higher walls.
Spied America,
flew there in mismatched shoes.

Spooled out the distance between us.
Years and years in phone cables,
e-mails, photographs.

I stayed behind. Toed the line.
Good Girl me.
Grew up,
got married,
bore children,
got sick.

Tom wasn't stumped.
His liquid reasoning
still floated obstacles.
There's one sure cure for nausea,
he phoned one afternoon.

And where would *I* find that?

Next day,
a parcel in my letterbox.

In the parcel, a small silver case.
In the small silver case,
six joints
neatly rolled.

And a note:

In the spirit of adventure,
this is from your brother Tom.

I Can't Walk On Water

I can't walk on water.
Skip like a stone across
this burning sea.
Can't even walk away from you,
your yawning arms.

Death is a pirate's ship
anchored on a calm horizon.
It's a limp cotton flag
on a windless sky.

They have knotted it
to my sharp, white bones.
I can raise one arm
– a watermark for the tide –
to show you how far, how deep it goes.

From shore you call to me
of hands that are dealt,
races that are stayed.
Of skill and hope and surgeons.

Sweetheart. Somewhere
I chose the wrong ladder,
slid down a snake,
failed to step over a crack.

And this is the penalty.
I must feel
each stinging slap,
each sharp-toothed

suck of undertow.
The tide must boil channels
around my stubborn thighs.

Your love, of course,
will well up like rough sand
or blood
between my clinging toes.

Nothing can save me from that.

Prayer

In his church is a lady called Maud.
Maud knows a lady called Grace,
and Grace
has a Madam who is ill.

That's why Mr Sneli is here.
In his 1986 Mercedes
he has travelled all
the way from Guguletu
to the foreign fields of Rondebosch
to pray over me.

By the way,
Grace has never called me Madam.
You, maybe,
or *Wena*.
Occasionally, *Ma*.

Later I go to find her.

*Who **is** this Mr Sneli?* I ask,
my scalp still powdered with ash,
my mind still jumbled with spells.

Grace leans into the ironing board.
It creaks sycophantically.
She doesn't even look up
as she mutters,

*That man can **pray**.*

For Thomas in California

Do you lie awake at night,
cousin Nolan asks,
and worry about your kids?
I knew someone else, he sighs,
She looked fine, just like you.
Until she died.

And the woman who cut my hair
at the hairdresser's in Cavendish Square.
She had an Aunt with the illness
who'd been one hundred percent OK.
Until six months ago.

Then there's the nurse in Wynberg,
who sews prosthetic pockets and enjoys
keeping me up to date with each fresh
death amongst her dwindling
customer-base.

I save them all up for you, Tom,
for Sunday nights when you phone
and I can finally fume,
I'm going to live
to bury all those people
who think I won't make it.

I wait for you to tell me,
Don't say that.
That's awful.
People don't **mean**
to be unkind.

But you just say,
Hand me that shovel, girl.
I'm gonna help you dig.

Kook en geniet
for Dr. H

On page thirty-two, he said, unsmiling,
you will find
the crunchie recipe.

Substitute half a cup butter
with half a cup
of finely grated herb.

Mix as instructed.
Bake in moderate oven
for thirty minutes.

Serve and enjoy!

They tasted no different
from normal crunchies,
but I relished the sight
of my sixty-seven-year old mother
measuring shredded *dagga*
into a china mixing bowl.

Later, I lay on my bed
watching purple flowers
explode on a white ceiling.

Alterations

Oophorectomy: *operation to remove both...ovaries (and)...stop making... oestrogen, which may be helping your cancer to grow...you may get some menopausal symptoms, such as hot flushes...© Breakthrough Breast Cancer*

The doctor says it will be
like shutting a door.

A house has been vandalised, say.
Windows shattered,
furniture smashed,
foreign footprints and the smell
of strange drugs smeared
across the hall and on up the passageway.

Once you've expelled all intruders
– the doctor says –
you set about mopping up the mess.
Righting furniture, barring windows,
bolting doors
and shooting all collaborators.

Through a keyhole in my navel,
they plan to unhook my turncoat ovaries
that were not making babies
but building cluster bombs
in my front yard.

Afterwards I will feel nothing.
A little stiffness in the shoulders perhaps.
There will be no oestrogen.
No cancer.

No worries.

Just a good clean house. A padlocked door.

And behind it the fires begin
their blind and livid burning.

It's Difficult to Explain

It's difficult to explain hot flushes.
Neither quotidian nor laughable,
they're God's curse on me
for having cancer,
cancer's curse on me
for forsaking God.

The experience loves me.

In the queue at Woolworths
I'm suddenly aflame.
Sweat oozes off me like lava.
I'm trapped in the core
of a silent volcano.

I want to crumble
like a white-ashed tree.

People look away.
A woman laughs
as if in sheepish solidarity.
How we women must suffer.
All of them are repelled
by my body's anarchy.

But the shop assistant
has completed a first aid course
for beginners.

She abandons her cash-register
and brings a glass of water.
She pulls out a chair,
and orders me to sit.

In her blue uniform
she kneels at my feet,
splits open the lapels
of my winter boots,
and peels off my
socks.

Her name,
in horizontal gold,
is Sibusizwe.

In her cool, clay-pot palms
she holds my feet
like new-laid eggs.

Christ.
Have mercy.

Tuesday is Rubbish Day

We park the bin
outside our front gate.
Soon, the rattle
of a stolen Woolworth's trolley.

From my bedroom window,
I watch a man with bare hands
open our wheeled black bin.

How like a surgeon he knows
what to take
and what to leave behind.

I'd Like to Say a Word

I'd like to say a word
about the ladies from
Reach For Recovery.

Firstly, these are no Amazons.
There's not one of them
would willingly have sawed or seared
their right breast off
in preparation for this war.

For weapons, rather
the kindness of tea-cups,
the gentle duelling
of ordinary or Rooibos,
and the hostessy circulation
of plattered words
you never dared try at home,

Recovery
Survival
A normal life.

August

She made a will.
Jewellery
books
a bicycle.
Songs she'd liked,
places she loved.

But the chief question stuck.
Fattening on her silence, it grew,
thick as a white worm

until the day she stood in a field,
propping her baby like a loaded gun
and watched her son running,
his feet shuddering in oversized gumboots.

He stopped,
and bowled a bunch
of pink Oxalis through the air.

Momma this is just like heaven!

Missing

I don't remember what
made her cry that day.
Her brother teasing?
Her sister ignoring her?
Running to where I sat
in the armchair of the sunny lounge.

That was before they allowed
a prosthesis to lie
over the healing scar
and I only remember
– long after she'd stopped –

how hard her skull felt
on the bones of my chest.

You Eat your Veg

You eat your veg,
smear on sunblock,
take omega-threes
and potassium in legal doses,
strap yourself in
and always lock the doors.

Shit still happens.

So I went to church.
I wanted a word.

What about my children?
I asked,
What about my husband
and the promises I made?
(In front of You,
if You care to remember).

The organ wheezed out
its squashed, sour notes.
My soliloquies swam up
to the musty beams
and were trapped.

Outside,
the white sun dissolved
like a wafer under my tongue.

I waited for an answer.
Weeks
months
years
a decade.

Crime Scene

Afterwards, some mornings
he'd catch me
sleeping, or lying,
– protected by pillows –
face down in a flash of sunlight
on our bedroom floor.

What was I doing,
he would rage.
This was not normal
or reasonable.

All he wanted was to have me back
sans cancer
sans cares
sans everything.

Flight SAA 346 To Johannesburg
for Emma

If my hand were as big as this plane
I could press it over the mouth
of the sun.

I could throw down rivers like shoelaces
to see how they land,
and swing my wide feet over cities
soldered to the earth
like circuits on a mother-board.

In ten strides I could be where you sit
behind your tiny desk
at your tiny school.

I could roll you in my palm
like a pearl.

I could keep you in a house
the size of my lunchbox.
With my lake-sized eyes
I could narrow you
into the wide portal of my pupils
and keep you there.

And at night
I could curl around you
like a mountain range
too steep to be crossed.

Recurral

Do you lie awake at night,
cousin Nolan wants to know,
and wonder if it will come back?

Like a dog that
once peed on a lamppost?

Yes.
No.

But sometimes I dream
it's 3 a.m. and my doorbell is ringing.

A taxi has been circling
my neighbourhood for years
and finally found

the right address.

Christmas Eve 1997

Bales of straw and
a three-man band
in the Kidd's Beach parking lot.

Cold-necked Castles,
Klippies and Coke,
everyone's backs to the sea.

Come, Emma,
you're too small to mind
if people stare, and I love it
when you laugh and grip
your baby thighs against
my jiving waist.
Come, Emma,
the music has us in its teeth
and it's shaking us round
the Kidd's Beach parking lot.

Glass half-empty still half-full,
little bit of living left behind
and my legs still move don't they
my arms still hold
I can hear
I can speak
I can see –

you,
for instance.
And those stars that just stood by
and let it all happen.
Even they've stopped

to watch us, to say,
At this stage, a little
insane indulgence can do no harm.
And those people
staring awkwardly
down at their drinks,

behind their backs the sea
wheezes and barks,
an old man ambushed by laughter.

Payback Poem: October 2008

I want to go back eleven years
to Cavendish Square,
and the apprentice stylist
who shaved off all my hair one afternoon.

Who set the razor so unwillingly
to a number four,
then eased it across my scalp
to liberate my long, thick hair

and afterwards
refused to let me pay.

I'd like to bring him here to 2008
to show him me, seated
in a hairdresser's chair
while my greying hair
gets snipped into a bob.

I want to meet his sad reflection
in the mirror,
to smile at him and say,

I suffered
but I survived.

Bequest

for Georgia

Not my headaches
or thin skin,
not the other
sinister genetic thing.

Just more of what
you already have:

laughter
good friends
my love
this poem.

December Poem

Year after year amongst the Christmas surfers,
your yellow T-shirt and boogie board
brazening it over the cheery-backed waves.

By December 31st that shirt is cardboard-stiff with salt.

Fashion doesn't drop anchor in your holiday mind.
That shirt's for comfort, and, we all know,
fun.

Life's not perfect, you seem to shrug,
righting yourself ashore,
then turning to drag
your bobbing board into the waves again.
Happiness? Impossible.
Like prising mussels bare-handed
from a rock.

Why not, then, wear a banana-yellow shirt,
harness a boogie board to a willing wave?
Why not wander, wet and blinking,
across the hot sand
in search of your glasses and a towel?

As for me, waiting by that towel,
holding your glasses in sandy hands,
why not give in and say,
as you always want me to,
how dear as salt you are to me?

Catch-22

We walk to dinner at Maureen's
though everyone says we shouldn't.
Not at night.
Not when gangsters roam the streets
with guns.

Look at us. Look how the rain
draws back in despair
while you march ahead with Ben,
his teenage takkies whispering
over dark puddles.

You never, I shout,
huddling Ben's sisters at my side.
Over hunched shoulders you yell back,
Of course I do.

At dinner I drink cider and ignore you.
I tell them all how hard,
how very very hard it's been
living with you these years.

But walking home at midnight
Ben recalls reading *Catch-22*.
In the middle of the silvered road he stops,
knee-capped by laughter.
His sisters stare, amazed.

Come walk by me. Hold my hand tight.
The August trees are wristing raindrops
like hawkers with fake Cartiers,

but the moon escapes their desperate fingers.
She holds our life in her hands!
Yet she bowls bravely on without
spilling a single
living
drop.

Poetry Class 2008: Write a Poem on the Theme of Breastfeeding

No.
I can't.
I never think of them.
Although there is one there
I never think of it.
There is a scar there
I do not touch it.
It is unloved, a razed
squatter camp,
a burnt circle where nothing else
will ever graze
or grow
again.

What I Plan

I plan to eat oat snaps (more than two),
while drinking Lady Grey tea
in a house at Plettenberg Bay
overlooking the mountains, and a sea
rolled flat as pastry by the fussy wind.

I plan to not-plan or anticipate
the abrupt scream of metal,
or the phone call at 3 a.m.,
or the silent busy-ness of my own
multiplying cells.

I plan to forgive myself if I do.

I plan to lose myself – often –
in the temporary,
heated or chilled,
to sit out the turbulence when it mauls
at the equator of my muscle and bone.

I plan to remember I've kept afloat till now.

And remembering better times, I plan
to call them once again to account,
to hang them from my warped mainsail
like worn and mended sails that shout,
Here you have held the wind.

Found

When I wasn't even looking.
This unexpected moment,
    this unpredicted shelf
my life built a ladder to reach.

Blue sea ochre sand,
green armbands for Emma.

I abandon shore. Lie back in the waves
and let the water discover me,

but the sea won't let me sink.

Rising on icy hind paws
she balances me high
on the tip of her nose,
a bright and shining ball.

Endnotes

Page 29   Walking to school again
Ons sal Afrikaans praat.
Ons sal oefen vir die toets (Afrikaans):
We'll talk Afrikaans.
We'll practise for the test.

Page 33   Grace by name
Madiba-like:
Nelson Mandela was known as "Madiba,"
the name of the Xhosa tribe to which he belonged.

Page 46   Prayer
Wena (Xhosa): You

Page 49   Kook en geniet
Kook en geniet (Afrikaans):
"Cook and Enjoy". A popular Afrikaans recipe-book.
dagga (Afrikaans): marijuana

Page 63   Christmas Eve 1997
Klippies (Colloquialism):
Abbreviation of "Klipdrift", a local brandy.

OTHER WORKS IN THE DRYAD PRESS LIVING POETS SERIES

AVAILABLE NOW

Otherwise Occupied, Sally Ann Murray
Landscapes of Light and Loss, Stephen Symons
An Unobtrusive Vice, Tony Ullyatt
A Private Audience, Beverly Rycroft
Metaphysical Balm, Michèle Betty

FORTHCOMING IN 2019

Allegories of the Everyday, Brian Walter
happier were the victims, Kambani Ramano

OTHER WORKS BY DRYAD PRESS (PTY) LTD

Unearthed: A selection of the best poems of 2016,
edited by Joan Hambidge and Michèle Betty
The Coroner's Wife: Poems in Translation, Joan Hambidge

Available in South Africa from better bookstores, internationally from
African Books Collective (www.africanbookscollective.com)
and online at www.dryadpress.co.za

DRYAD PRESS
People! Read Poetry

Printed in the United States
By Bookmasters